"Teach A Man To Fish"

I0454828

Peter LeGrove

This Is My Story About Helping A Homeless Man Make Enough Money To Survive In Hanoi Vietnam

Disclaimer

Although the author and publisher have made every effort to ensure that the information in this book was correct at press time, the author and publisher do not assume and hereby disclaim any liability to any party for any loss, damage, or disruption caused by errors or omissions, whether such errors or omissions result from negligence, accident, or any other cause.

This book is for entertainment purposes only. The views expressed are of the author alone and should not be taken as expert advice. The reader is responsible for his own actions. Neither the author or the publisher assume any liability or responsibility on behalf of the reader or purchaser of this material.

You must use common sense when helping out Homeless people in a strange country, The author and publisher assume no liability or responsibility for any accidents or anything that happens to you, while reading or following this book. The author is not a licensed Aid Worker in any country in the world, he is an author writing about what he did to help a homeless person in Vietnam.

The author and publisher claim no responsibility for results obtained while following this book as everybody is different and are starting at different levels. You the reader are responsibility for your actions and safety while trying to help out homeless people in Vietnam or any other country for that matter.

Your Free Book

As a way of saying thank you for buying my book I'm offering you a free book.

This book "How To Add Qualifications To Your CV Using FREE Courses" is about what you can learn over the internet for free. It shows you where to go to get Certificates of Accomplishment that you can add to your CV.

Click here and you will be taken to another page where you can download the free book.

Get Your FREE book here
http://animalsdinosaursandbugs.com/MOOC-download.html

Who Will Benefit From This Book

This little book is from my experience trying to help a homeless person just make enough money to survive. I'm not an aid worker nor have I had any experience in social work. I go to church where I am quite involved and that is about the limit to my experience. It just happened where this guy I knew got fired and our paths kinda crossed.

This book could be helpful to people working in developing countries, like Missionaries and aid workers. Or even to people in the developed world dealing with the homeless. Here people who know what to do and have done it before, could see where I went wrong or what I should have done. I was making it up as I went along.

It could be beneficial to social workers, to give them an insight into how people in other countries survive without a safety net. And they could see that the homeless situation is the same in many countries. My man Van was homeless because he had to be, he just didn't have enough money to pay rent, so he chose to live on a park bench. If he had enough money he would go back to live in the boarding house. He was not homeless because he wanted to be.

Also people involved in sales and marketing could see the timeless wisdom past down from the legends of marketing, still applies when you are homeless and living on a park bench. And the bottom line is if you want to better yourself you have to put in the effort and the time as well as learn from the masters.

How To Use This Book

First read the book to see what I did, then work out what you would do. Think about what I did and decide if you would do the same. My main challenge was getting my homeless man to see things differently then do things differently.

If you are into marketing, then you could have a look at the resources I used to see if you could incorporate them into your program. To be honest if I didn't already have a background in marketing and sales I would have been walking blind. At least I had an understanding of what he needed to do to survive. But for me to get him to do the things I mentioned it was impossible. He just didn't have the motivation or the desire to change.

You would have to look at the background of your homeless person as well as the background he lived in. So you would know what you are up against. Also you might have to learn new skills. I didn't do anything to try and find out how to help homeless people. I have all the information out there at my fingertips but I never searched for anything to help. I'm not trying to say I know it all, I knew I had only two weeks left on my visa, so I was a bit pushed for time.

What Is In This Book

Learn From The Masters

Change The Headline Until It Works

Van Just Would Not Try To Do New Things

You Should Look At The Teacher

Time Traveling

Van Was Now On His Own

Looking Back

This Is My Story

Hi. My name is Peter LeGrove and while I was teaching English in Hanoi, Vietnam, I had an opportunity to try and help a homeless person try and better himself. I have had no experience at all with anything to do with homeless people. The closest I got, was when I was nearly down and out myself, with very little money coming in. I was trying to make enough money to live on, selling stuff in the street markets. At those times I used to eat the free lunch at the church. There I was surrounded by every homeless derelict from miles around. But they were good people and they looked after each other, and the church helped them out, as best it could. Another church I went to, handed out a leaflet that explained what you could get from the government. As the government tried its hardest to make sure you didn't know these things. On the leaflet, was a list of all the free and very cheap places you could go to eat cheap, and I used to live amazingly Cheap In An UnCheap World.

Anyway being homeless in the West is a lot different from being homeless in South East Asia. At least in the West you do get some government handouts, but they are not very much. In Asia you get nothing. My old friend in the West was on the pension, and he lived in a van in a covered parking garage. During working time the garage was full, but after work and on the weekends he had the place to himself. The pension in some countries is not very much, and this is how my friend could live on the pension. The pension for two people living together under the same roof is reasonable, but when one passes away the amount of money coming in is halved, and that is when the money problems start. As my friend found out, so he sold his house and now lives in a van.

Property Taxes Are Expensive

In the West if you own your own home then you have to pay property taxes, and these taxes are not cheap. Of all my monthly expenses, property taxes were the most expensive. The internet and phone was usually about $120 a month, electricity about the same depending on the weather, and property taxes came in at a whopping $200 a month. I didn't even spend that much on food. Also you had to pay tax on the car, but that was a very cheap tax coming in at somewhere between $10 and $15 dollars a month. My friend in the garage had to pay $100 a month rent for the parking space, plus the tax on the car, which could come in at closer to $25 dollars a month when everything was added in. With two people paying the bills you could survive, but as soon as the income was halved you could get into financial difficulties very easily, as my mother found out when dad died.

Anyway in Asia there is no safety net, so after my friend got fired he was on his own. And this is my story about how I tried to help him stay alive. It is not easy living in a dog eat dog world, especially when you are trying to etch out an existence at the bottom end of the social ladder, where people are very protective of their turf, because it is where they made the money to live on. And the last thing they wanted was somebody else moving in. Even though my friend was a long way from taking over their territory, and it didn't take them long to realize he was not a threat.

What We Were Up Against

There is an old saying from I don't know where, that basically says "Buy a man a fish and you feed him for a day. Teach a man to fish and you feed him for a lifetime" Very true, but can it be done. I was stuck in Hanoi, Vietnam teaching English. Good city, good people, but rip off merchants everywhere, and it is one of these tourist places where there seems to be an atmosphere of contempt towards tourists. I had the feeling we were cash cows just waiting to be milked. But all around in this city there were people who genuinely liked the foreigners. And I seemed to gravitate towards these people. Like some shops I wouldn't go in, unless the serving girl that I thought was very pleasant was on the counter.

Just as an example I live off vitamins. I take vitamins all the time, so when I got food poisoning I went and brought some Vitamin C. You can buy a little blister packet with 10 pills in it. The first shop charged me 20,000 dong which is just under $1 U.S. I had no idea what the price should be, so I brought them. When I ran out I went to another shop and brought the same packet, plus a blister pack of Magnesium and both together cost 20,000 dong, so I asked how much the Vitamin C was and it cost 5,000 vnd. That is when I realised I had been screwed. Anyway when I ran out this time, I went to another shop, and the price for both the Vitamin C and the Magnesium came to 55,000 dong for both, so I walked out. The shop assistant could see I had brought the same pills before, and she slapped on her commission. To some people you are just a milk cow. Anyway in the little shop off the main road and away from the hospital, the price for both the Vitamin C and the Magnesium came to 19,000 dong, and the Vitamin C was 4,000 dong. So she had a customer for the whole time I was there, plus any other foreigner I steered in her direction.

This is typical of the atmosphere we were living in. And in this atmosphere, I befriended this old guy who used to park motorbikes. That was his job for 14 hours a day plus lunch, and he wasn't very good at it, from what I could see. He used to spend most of his time asleep on a bike he had just parked. But he could ramble on in English, but he couldn't understand anything I said. And half the time I couldn't understand what he was going on about. To say the least, he had a few screws loose, but he was a nice old man. And in a world of living in backpacker hostels, where you have instant friends who come and go, having a long term friend is unusual.

How To End Up Living In A Park

Anyway he ended up getting fired. I wasn't overly surprised, as I would have either fired him a long time ago or retrained him. Here in Asia retraining is a thing of the future. I could see things he could do but he just didn't, whether he wasn't allowed too or he didn't think to do them, I don't know. Anyway he rang me to tell me he had been fired, so we arranged to meet in the garden around the old Hoan Kiem Library. It turned out this was his new home. He used to sleep on the park benches at night, under the stars. Except when it rained and then he would sleep under a canopy. While he was working he used to live in a boarding house, but with no income he had to leave. And that is how he ended up in the garden.

This garden was one of my favorite places in Hanoi Vietnam. I used to go there in the mornings for my morning exercises, on the days I didn't have morning class. Before I used to run around Hoan Kiem Lake, but there were just too many people, and this little garden was the best kept secret in Hanoi. So in the mornings, I would run around the garden, do my morning exercise routine, which consisted of 20 squats, 20 lunges, 10 pushups, 10 leg raises and 10 crunches. Then I would run around the garden and do my exercise routine all over again. I used to do this three times and sometimes four, before I was too tired to move. Then I would walk back to my hostel for a shower.

Food And Water

And he was there every morning and lunchtime when I went to have my lunch. And he was broke, so I would take him to a small, cheap, buffet style restaurant and buy him lunch. These buffet style restaurants were really good. In the glass cabinet there were many plates of food. They would put a pile of rice on a plate, and you pointed to what you wanted, and they would tell you the price. Or you would tell them you wanted 25Kvnd, and they would tell you when you had enough food on your plate. There were three prices 20K, 25K and 30K. I would buy 25K for me and 20K for the old man. That is about $1 U.S. Mine was just over $1 and his was under. Anyway he got a feed a day.

His name was Van, and he had no idea how to live cheap, other than sleeping on a park bench. Years of backpacking around the globe, had taught me how to live cheap and reasonable healthy. Even though when I was teaching, I had more money than I could spend. So I took him down the supermarket, and brought a loaf of fresh bread for 9K, and a small tin of sardines for 10K. That would be enough to live off for one day. It might not be very healthy, but he would not be too hungry. The oil in the sardines would see to that, as well as the bread. So he had to make 20K per day just to survive. This is the "Give a man a fish, and you feed him for a day," and that is all I was doing. I had to teach him how to fish, so he would make enough money to survive.

Also water was something else you need everyday, especially in summer in the tropics, where the temperature could hit the high 30s very easily. A one and a half liter plastic bottle of water, ran somewhere between 8,000 and 10,000vnd. So to get clean water you had to pay for it. Van wasn't into paying for water, as he didn't have enough money, so he used to get the water from the tap in the toilet. Something I would never do. Anyway I showed him how to sterilize the water using the sun. That is you put the water in a clear plastic bottle, and you leave it in the sun as long as you can, turning occasionally. This way the ultra violet rays from the sun, kill the bugs in the water. Van thought it was a dumb idea, as the water heated up in the sun, and the last thing you wanted was hot water to drink. So he never did it. He brought a packet of white sugar, and he would put a slice of lemon and some sugar in the water bottle. Whether this was flavoring or it helped kill the bugs I don't know. Sugar is a good sterilizer, but you usually have to use it in large doses.

Stomach Problems

Anyway I ended up with severe diarrhea, and I don't know where I got it. When you live in the tropics in the middle of summer, it is very easy to pick up something. When you eat any food that has been sitting behind a glass cover in the sun, it doesn't take long for the bad bugs to multiply. I hope I never picked it up from Van. In the middle of summer, with the daytime temperature running in the high 30's, you need to drink lots of water, and I did. And when you have severe diarrhea, you have to drink more, and I did. I was knocking back Vitamin C in large doses, like 1000 mgs a time, five times a day, and garlic to try and control it, but it got the better of me. I didn't know what I had eaten or picked up, but I couldn't shake it. I tried a couple of different brands of food poisoning medicine, and they didn't stop it. So I took a round of stomach worm pills, and they had no effect. I checked the internet and couldn't find very much there. I thought it might be Giardia, but you can get that anywhere, and I was not sick enough for that. I don't think it was amebic dysentery, I had that in the Sahara and I was not that sick. When I had that, I lost so much weight I was putting extra holes in my belt, so I could keep my pants up. That is how much weight I lost. This was something new all I had was diarrhea, nothing else. I could still run around the garden and do my morning exercises. Mind you I didn't feel like doing them, but I did. I just walked around with a wad of toilet paper stuffed up my butt, just in case. I just had to plan when to eat. If I had morning class I didn't eat in the mornings at all. For evening classes I would just eat lunch, and that was it till after class. I was hoping my body would sort it out, but so far it is over two weeks now, and it hasn't.

When You Are Homeless How Do You Make Money

To help Van make some money, I mentioned becoming a beggar. There were very few beggars in our part of town. Actually I was only stopped by one beggar, the whole time I was there. She would walk up to me with a Vietnamese hat, and stick in under my nose, while I was at the bus stop. And she had a fair amount of money in the hat, enough to keep her in food for a few days. But there must be some sort of stigma against begging, as Van would rather starve than beg. I wanted to show him the beggar women, but our paths never crossed when I was with him. I've never been a beggar, and I've never considered doing it, but then again I have never been completely down and out. I must admit in my country, begging is on the rise. An accumulation of taxes and inflation and the hand out mentality. And we are an OECD country, but that means nothing nowadays. Asia is the next superpower. We in the West are going backwards, and Asia is where it is all happening. But Van wouldn't think so, sleeping under the stars on his very own park bench.

He used to talk about one time when a church charity was handing out food, and he had the best feed of his life. This happened before, when he was down and out many years ago. And he was hoping it would happen again. But since he never went to church, and I had never seen any church charities handing out anything, I doubted if that would ever happen. Around Christmas something like that might happen, but in my years in Asia I had never seen it. Val still hoped it would happen again. I think that happened when he was a kid, growing up in the backstreets of Hanoi. And now all he had was me, and I was doing it because I had no one to eat lunch with. Living in backpacker hostels you have 'instant friends' that come and go all the time. How can you not have 'instant friends,' when you are living in a dorm surrounded by people.

Hoan Kiem Cathedral

The big church, the Catholic Cathedral, was something else. It was old, very old, and looking at it from the outside, it looked very old. But inside it was immaculate. It was a beautiful church. I would go on the weekends, even though I didn't understand a word that was said, it was beautiful. Also it was very crowded. And if you were not properly dressed, like your shoulders were not covered, they would turn you away. And they turned away a lot of foreigners. Someone should tell the people at the church, in the West we have serious problems trying to get people to go to church, and turning them away doesn't help. Anyway when Van was working, he worked on one side of the Cathedral, and I lived on the other side, so that is how we met. I used to walk past him on the way to the garden, to the bus stop and to my school. And he liked speaking English so he spoke to me, and I use to talk to him everyday. This church was a magnet for foreigners I have never seen so many people in a church. In China I thought the churches were crowded, but they were nothing compared to here.

Life Of A Professional Shoe Polisher

So what could Van do to get some money? Doing a labor job would not suit him, as he was getting old and was not very strong. So I asked him what he could do, and he said he could polish shoes. Now that is a good idea. So he took me down to a polish shoe shop, and I brought him some polish and some brushes. Cost around 70K vnd, a very cheap business to start, but if you are in business you have to work, and that was the problem, he didn't like work. Van had no idea how to start a business, or how to adjust to make some money. And now he was all set to become a Professional Shoe Polisher, but could he do it. So I left him to it, hoping it would work out for him.

The first day he made 20K, just enough to live on very cheaply. I figured it had to get better. Anyway we still had lunch together, so at least he had something to eat. The next day was worse, he didn't make anything. So I left him to it, to see if things got better. If he made any money he would go down to a really cheap local supermarket, where they sold stuff people didn't want to buy, or very out of date stock. Here you could buy bread that had been fried and put in a packet for 6,000vnd. I eat most things, but this I would not eat. For 9,000vnd I would buy fresh bread, but Van couldn't see the difference.

Anyway nothing was regular, and he made anywhere between nothing and 5,000vnd a day. Here I was making 500K a day for 6 days a week. And he couldn't even make 5,000 a day consistently. But the problem was, my visa was running out, and I had less that two weeks, to get Van into a money making position. In the mornings after my run, we would walk back to the lake, and I would leave him there. From what he said he was not allowed to work around the lake. Which is probably right as I was never stopped by a shoe polisher while on the lake shore. Even though there were people selling everything to the many tourists. Even when I was walking home, covered in sweat with my running shoes on, rather ambitious shoe polishers, tried to polish my running shoes. I would never let them as the shoes were not leather, and they didn't need polishing. I would clean them quite regularly. Anyway I had my own personal, shoe polisher.

What Was Van Not Doing

Anyway I had to intervene here with Van, to see what was really going on. So I went for a walk with him, to see what the situation was really like. We passed people polishing shoes at 7 o'clock in the morning, while at the bus stop. Van called these people 'Professional Shoe Polishers' and I said what are you? 'You have to become a Professional Shoe Polisher.' Now the first rule in business is to do something you love to do. If you don't love what you are doing, forget it, you are not going to put your heart and soul into it, as Van was not doing. That was problem number one – He didn't like doing what he was doing. My new mantra now was, "Polish or starve." I was very disappointed in him he was just leaving money on the table. I would point out people with shoes that needed polishing, and he would have some lame excuse for not asking them. He was the problem.

Also I had to get Van on the street earlier to polish shoes. The other Professional Shoe Polishers were out there while I was going for a run. And I usually started somewhere between 6 and 6:30 am. Van would be sitting on a park bench, until we walked to the lake, and there he would sit on another bench. I don't know what time he started polishing, but I know it was not too early. And I had to try and get him up earlier. You know "The early bird catches the worm" but I couldn't. I showed him the other Professional Shoe Polishers, all out there polishing shoes for people going to work. All he said was, "They are Professional Shoe Polishers," and that was it. He had this thing about not stopping people walking down the street. Yet the other Professional Shoe Polishers tried to stop me. Maybe he had a bad experience with one person he tried to stop on the street before.

As I could figure out, the shoe polishing situation looked something like this. The Professional Shoe Polishers, all had cafes where they polished shoes, and they would polish the security guards shoes for free. Now the security guard would keep all the other shoe polishers away. And I must admit there were many shoe polishers around the city. Most cafes had one. So how was Van going to fit in. I walked down one street with may cafes and there were no polishers. So I sent Van there and he still got nothing.

Why Not Try The Foreigner Market

Then I told him what to say in English, to the many tourists walking around. I heard him say something to one foreigner, but he didn't polish any shoes so that didn't work out. Anyway I told him to say "Excuse me, would you like your shoes polished for 10,000 Vietnamese Dong" (the local currency). This way he was saying the price, and he was not trying to rip off the foreigners, which the other shoe polishers usually did. The main problem was he could not understand what anybody said in English. He learned English by reading, so if anybody said anything, I told him to say, "It will take about 5 minutes," and hoped that answer would help. Anyway I don't know if he ever tried it out, but I hope he did. If he could break into the foreigner market, he would be all set up. When I was saying anything important to Van, I had to write it down, as he just didn't understand anything I said.

He was not a rip off merchant, he was rather very honest and very gullible. He had a phone at one stage, but it ran out of charge, and instead of asking me to charge it back up, he just hung onto it. Some guy came up to him, and asked if he could borrow his phone to send a text. Van said the battery had run out, so the guy said he would take it over to the security office, and ask them to charge it. So Van said yes, and never saw his phone or the guy again. He went over to the security office and asked them, and they didn't know what he was talking about. Anyway the security people knew him and me, and they did their very best to get rid of him. In the rain he used to sit under the canopy, so the security guards rolled it up, so there was hardly any canopy to sit under. So when it rained Van had to stand, as there was not enough cover to lie down.

Living In The Garden

There was one serious advantage about living in the garden, and that was, there was a free toilet. The only free toilet in a city where it usually cost 2,000 to 4,000 vnd to go to the toilet. There was a very old lady, who also spent lunch time in the garden, and she usually cleaned the toilet. She used to pick up rubbish and sell it to the recyclers. I saw her once in the night market, dragging a large cardboard box back to her stash. I asked if she wanted a hand, and she said no, so I walked away. I would say having a foreigner helping an old lady, wouldn't go down to well with the locals. Especially in this dog eat dog world. In the garden she would check the rubbish bins for bottles to sell to the recyclers. I don't know how much money she made, and she had the system down to a fine art. She used to come in at lunch time with a take away box of food, very similar to what me and Van used to eat in the restaurant. I don't know where she got it or how much it cost. Anyway I offered her some lychees after I brought a couple of kilos, and after that she would offer me any extra food she had.

There were always women selling fried bread rolls. I didn't like the bread. Since they walked the street they used to use the free toilet, and the old women would look after their basket of bread. And for this she would get some bread rolls. So the old women would give me some, and made it quite clear I was not to give them to Van. I don't know why she didn't like him but I had a fair idea. And it had to do with his psychological problems. He would always talk about himself. Anyway I would buy her some biscuits from the supermarket, and we had a little thing going where we would trade food.

Street People

On the street there were women, who would carry vegetables and fruit around on big trays attached to a pole, they carried on their shoulder. There was a tray in front and one behind to balance the load. These women never seemed to get it with foreigners. We were milk cows and they were their own worst enemy. Foreigners who brought from these sellers, usually didn't buy because they wanted what they were selling. They were buying from these sellers to help them out and to lessen their load. And these sellers did everything they could, to make sure we went back to the supermarket where we belonged. For a start they would never give you any change. They would load up what you wanted instead of giving change, and when I took off what they had added to the pile, they would be very reluctant to give me change. And when they did, it was always less than what it should have been. There were exceptions here, like the pineapple seller on the corner by the Buddhist temple near the church. She had mastered the art of being nice and honest, and the foreigners always were back to buy pineapples from her. She never worried about a customer. But there were very few like her. Beside her sat a fried bread seller, who used to go to the garden, and was friends with the old lady. I always meant to buy some bread off her, but I just didn't like the bread. Anyway I could have given it to Van. He was always starving.

Also after living in Hanoi for any length of time, you get desensitized to all the crap going on around you. And I ended up just going to the places where I didn't get ripped off. So it was quite difficult for me to buy something off a new seller. Some sellers just couldn't work it out. I like the sugar cane drink which is all over South East Asia, and even here some would try and up the price. All they were doing was making sure I never went back.

Cheap Cigarettes And Expensive Cigarettes

Here in Hanoi cigarettes are very cheap, around 10Kvnd for a cheap packet of 20. That is less than 50 cents US, so I didn't mind him smoking. That was very different from my country where a packet of cigarettes could knock you back 400,000 vnd. As most foreigners found out, the hardest thing to do when they got back to their home country, is giving up cigarettes. Going from 50 cents a packet, to anything from $5 to $50 depending on which country you live in, was just too much.

Old habits die hard. When Van made 50,000 vnd one day, he went and brought a can of beer. He never considered saving a bit of extra cash for a rainy day. And here during the rainy season Van couldn't shine shoes, because they were wet. Even though the other Professional Shoe Polishers were out there drying the shoes before polishing them. Also with Van, cigarettes came before food. As soon as he made 10,000 vnd, he would run off and buy a packet of the cheapest cigarettes out there.

Demonizing cigarettes is one of the dumbest things the West has ever done. Sugar and booze has killed more people and cost more in health care than cigarettes ever did or ever will. They go on about secondhand smoke. What about secondhand booze, all the car accidents, fights and family violence. They have cost the taxpayer a lot more than the few who have been affected by secondhand smoke. And what about secondhand sugar. Diabetes and most metabolic diseases are caused by sugar. Cancer feeds off sugar, but it is still freely available with no special tax, and so is booze but it is taxed. With demonizing cigarettes, all the government has successfully managed to do, is drop more people below the poverty line, as a lot of people who can't afford to smoke, smoke. Also, I am sure it has increased family violence. In my country there are big billboards "Family Violence Is Not OK In …….. (the name of your town or city). I gave up when cigarettes were five dollars a packet and those billboards were not there then. Demonizing cigarettes is destroying our society. I'm sure it is a negative tax. When you put in the increase in family violence, and the increase in poverty, the amount of money they receive from the tax, does not cover the expenditure in family violence or poverty. We call it poverty at the check-outs, where a women with three kids, buys a loaf of bread for a $1, and a packet of cigarettes for over $30. You know those kids are starving. Schools now provide breakfast for their students. That is most likely an offshoot from the cigarette tax. The government lives in a different world from the people they look after. And all Van is trying to do, is make an honest living polishing shoes, but I somehow think he is his own worst enemy.

Park People

In the mornings when I do my morning exercises, there are a number of people who go there every morning. There was the group of old and not so old women, who do their morning exercise routine, in the same place every morning. There was usually around ten of them. Sometimes a very fit middle aged man would lead them, and other times a very fit middle aged women would be the leader. In between these were the badminton players and a few other runners like myself. The badminton players were a family, brother, sister, and mother and father. They would play badminton on the corner, near where I stopped to do my exercises. The young sister was the only other person to talk to me. Also there were a couple of old men who had had strokes, and they always walked around the park as best they could. And another old guy who used to walk around the garden quite fast, while I ran around him.

Also a security guard would come in at lunchtime, to sleep on what I called his bench. He was very young, probably around 20 years old, and he worked 14 hours a day or night. Even though we are regulation mad in the west, sometimes the regulations do help us, like we don't work 14 hours a day.

This is just an example of how Van couldn't see other people. When the security guard came in, I would have to tell Van to get off his seat and move to another seat. Van never thought to move himself. Sometimes I would come in late, and Van would be sitting on the security guard's seat, and the guard would be asleep on another bench. We were the regulars, and I used to see them as I walked around the streets, near my hostel and the big church. The garden brought us together, and believe it or not we used to look out for each other.

In the garden there was another old man that used to live there, but Van would not talk to him, or was it the other way round. Most of the security guards tolerated us, except for one. There is always somebody in uniform that tries to abuse their position, and this guy usually tried to move us on. The rest were good. One of them even offered Van a laboring job, but he never took it, it was too much like hard work. Anyway Van knew what he could do, and heavy labor work was not something he could do. He was not strong enough, and he was getting on in years. He was 58 years old, 10 years older than me. And he would sit on the park bench, and smoke while I ran around and did my exercises.

Training the Untrainable

I tried to get Van to do a one hour turn around in the cafes and restaurants. Most people would stay for an hour, so he should see new people every hour. He just couldn't see how this would help him. I was getting very frustrated, and my time was running out. I would have to leave very soon. I thought I might be the problem, so I stopped taking him to lunch, hoping hunger would be a good motivator. It wasn't, he just went hungry. I started taking him to lunch every other day. Anyway I was running out of time, as I had things to do before I left. It got to the stage, where we would walk different streets in the morning and after lunch. I had to see what it was like out there on the street. And it was not good.

I remembered a program from TV, "Filthy Rich and Homeless." It was reality TV, where a very rich person was paired with a homeless person, and lived their lifestyle for a while. In one episode a wealthy businessman was paired with this guy, who was not overly motivated to do anything, except sit in the pub and somehow try to get free beers. And the businessman tried to set him up to make some money, but the guy just didn't want to do anything. The businessman was visibly disappointed in the guy. He just could not understand why this guy didn't want to better himself. I was in the same type of situation. Van just didn't want to do anything, or didn't know how. He was so wrapped up in his past, he couldn't move forward. He would ask a few people and give up.

Learn From The Masters

Anything to do with selling is a numbers game. You have to ask so many to make so much money. Listen to 'Brian Tracy on Selling' and he will tell you that you need to know your numbers. And that is, how many sales you make from how many calls. So you can work out how many calls you need to make, to buy what you want. Van never got past the asking bit. Yet the other shoe polishers were always asking. I was walking round in brightly colored running shoes, and they would ask me. And these guys were the same as Van, but the big difference was they were Professional Shoe Polishers as Van would call them, and he did not think of himself as a Professional Shoe Polisher. I don't know what he thought of himself as, but he had a self image problem, very low self esteem.

Harry Brown in his masterpiece best seller that was published after his death by his wife "Secret of Selling Anything" based his selling on finding the right person. That is finding a person who wanted what you had to offer, and had the money to pay for it. Even Brian Tracy went on at length, about how to ask questions to determine whether the person standing in front of you, was a good prospect or not. Now that was the easiest part of Van's job, all he had to do was look at shoes, to see which needed cleaning. And then ask the person. Most people who had shoes that needed polishing, could afford 10,000vnd. Buses were 7,000vnd. But Van could not quite get to the asking stage. All Van had to do was follow Brian Tracy and Harry Brown's advice, and he should be able to make a living. Two selling greats, one from the past and other is probably the greatest selling guru alive today, and hopefully Van would survive. But there was one glaring problem, Van did not want to be a Professional Shoe Polisher. And the only way to change that was to come up with another profession, and I didn't have enough time for that.

Change The Headline Until It Works

According to the marketing masterminds, like Dan Kennedy, Ted Nicholas, and Clayton Makepeace, as well as the marketing legends from the past, like Elmer Wheeler, David Ogilvy and Claude C Hopkins, if your headline is not working, change it. And that is one thing I couldn't get Van to change. He said the same thing over and over again, even though it didn't work very well. Anyway why say something different from what everybody else was saying.

Some of the headlines I came up in English, he just couldn't seem to translate.

"Would you like the shiniest shoes in the cafe" "It will just take a moment"

"Would you like your shoes as striking as your business clothes" "It will just take a moment while you are eating"

"Your dull shoes do not suit your clothes, would you like me to shine them for you, it will only take a moment"

Van could have said a different line a day to see which one was better, but he preferred the standard "Would you like your shoes polished" that all the polishers were saying. So he never stood out in the crowd, he just faded into the background, where he liked to be.

Motivational speeches were useless on him. Tony Robbins wouldn't get very far with this guy. Tony could model his actions and have a very relaxing time sleeping on a park bench. I spent most of my life getting into personal development and trying to better myself, but I was not prepared for Van. Some people just can't get it together and Van lived in the past, whether it was a real past or an imaginary past I will never know.

Van Just Would Not Try To Do New Things

I tried to get him to sit at the front of the garden near the road, and if a potential customer walking past the garden, Van could say "I could polish your shoes while you sit in the shade in the garden, it will only take a moment." But Van never moved from his position on the park bench, at the back of the garden where nobody walked, and the few who did Van never asked.

I was thinking of bringing in some very simple personal development, by asking Van to do some very simple affirmations. I stopped short here as I was having problems getting him to do simple stuff that could make a difference in his life. And asking him to do affirmations might be just a little out of his depth,

Just simple stuff like "I like myself as I am."

"I like polishing shoes"

And Tony Robbins favorite "Every day in every way I am getting better and better"

I don't really know how Van would understand all this, and I figured he wouldn't bother doing these affirmations, so I didn't mention them. I must admit I do say Tony Robbins affirmation quite a lot, but obviously not enough.

In one of Zig Ziglar's tape sets from years ago, I think it was "Secrets Of Closing The Sale," Zig tells the story of the shoe shine man, who polished his shoes at a station somewhere. According to Zig this man was a real Professional Salesman. Everything he did and said was to get added value from the sale. From the way he squeaked the shoes, to how he could read a person from the clothes he was wearing. Now if Van could model this Professional Shoe Polisher we might get somewhere.

Now I don't like to say this, but Van was his own worst enemy. If I took any Vietnamese friends to meet Van, he would ramble on about his past. And in a very short time put them off, as he was always talking about himself. I shouldn't complain, after living in Hanoi for three months, the only friends I had was Van and the other people in the park.

You Should Look At The Teacher

And I shouldn't go on about Van. I was in his country so I didn't know the unspoken rules. And I couldn't speak the language. Also it is a communist country, so there are rules we don't have in the West. And to be honest, I have never been a shoe shine man, or done anything that resembled that line of work. I was a teacher with two failed businesses under my belt, and my writing career was barely breaking even. I was teaching because I liked it and it brought in a bit of money. But that also broke even with the plane tickets added in. The only time I made more money than breaking even with teaching, was when I was teaching online. This was steady income but I hated it, I preferred teaching live in a classroom.

I also should not be the person to get Van up and running, as I failed at selling many times. I always wanted to be a salesman, so I read the books and did the courses, but in the field I never made it. A line from the same Zig Ziglar course, Zig said something like "Zig the Salesman was ready." Before that Zig was a failure, and I was trying to have that moment in my life and say the same thing about me, but so far I never have.

Dan Kennedy from Magnetic Marketing said something like "It's taken me 5 years to become an overnight success." So far for me it is closer to 20 years, and I am still nowhere near being a success.

Time Traveling

As my time to leave the country was getting closer, my mantra of "polish or starve" got louder. But Van was undeterred. He used to go on about the worst time in his life, where he lived off a slice of bread a day. He was mentally preparing himself for the time ahead. He was doing what the "Choose Yourself" guy James Altucher would call "Time Traveling." Van was already planning a future without food. He was always time traveling, mainly to the past but now to the future. He never lived in the present. He would always go on about something that had happened in his past. But he never connected the dots, to how that was affecting his situation now, in the present. What did worry me was, he was already time traveling to his demise. I had to say to him many times "You are only 58 years old, you have a good 20 years left, so get with it." "Look at the old women, she must be 80 and she is still going." but I think my words fell on deaf ears. I must admit when I stopped time traveling, and starting living in the present my life improved.

Van Was Now On His Own

Anyway it was time for me to leave the country. I finished my evening adult class and walked back to the garden around 9:15, but Van was not there. My adult night school was just around the corner from the garden, the Cathedral, and my hostel. So I lived in a very good spot. And I used to drop into the garden on the way home from school. I had already put a packet of small bills together, so Van would have something to keep him going, for a week or two. I was not like "Rich Dad" from the "Rich Day Poor Dad" series of books, who would not give Robert Kyosaki any money when he was flat broke, and living in his car. In that instant, it was probably a good thing, as Robert went on to greater things, and very possibly changed the world as we know it. But Van was not going to change the world or his world any time soon, so I had some money ready to help him along the way.

I had asked two foreigners to look in on him, to see if he was doing OK, but I'll have to get them on facebook to find out if he is alright. One was a Frenchman, who worked on the Vietnamese stock market for a Hong Kong company. He used to stay in Hanoi during the week, and fly back to Hong Kong on the weekends to see his family. He would run around the garden occasionally, but he was not a regular, and he would not stay there for very long in the mornings. I usually stayed for about an hour. The other was the most unreliable person on the planet. I had arranged for him to take over some of my classes, but he never quite got around to getting to the classes. I even arranged to take him to the classes on the bus, but he couldn't make it. These were my part time classes and they paid after class, and he was broke, but instant money was not a motivator. My main night school paid monthly, into my bank account.

My bus to China was leaving at 7 in the morning, so I left my hostel around 6 o'clock and never saw Van again. I'll see him when I come back to Vietnam, in the next couple of months. Either he will be a skeleton or a Professional Shoe Polisher or something else.

Looking Back

That was my excursion into the world of trying to help a homeless man survive, in a country where there is no safety net, provided by the tax payer. It just goes to show in the West we are pretty pampered. And I doubt if many of our welfare recipients, would be able to survive if the safety net was taken away. But then again a bit of the money goes into taxes, and other government funded bills we have to pay.

Here trying to help Van I was up against my limitations. I was trying to get him to do something I had failed at a number of times. And that is selling or being a salesman. I had read the books and done the courses, but in the field I didn't make it. I know the fundamentals, and I am a teacher so I implanted my knowledge onto Van, but I couldn't implant experience as I didn't have any.

Also with Van I was up against his limitations, which were a major part of the problem. He had a severe self esteem problem that basically controlled his life. And I think he thought everybody was better than him. That is why he called the other shoe shine people, Professional Shoe Polishers, and he never referred to himself as a Professional Shoe Polisher. And I think that was his number one problem. He didn't like the job therefore he never put his heart and soul into it.

He had no empathy for the other people etching out an existence in the garden. He didn't think that way. He had a security guard ID, but I don't think he ever showed the other security guards his ID, and asked them if they could help him get a job. He showed me but I couldn't help him.

Looking back, I'm not really sure if I would change anything, except maybe give up on the 'Give a man a fish and you feed him for a day.' He relied on me to feed him, and that was a big part of the problem. He knew even if he made no money he would still get some food. Next time, if there is a next time, I should be more like "Rich Dad" and leave him up to himself to make it.

As an afterthought my problem with diarrhea did not get any better. In China I tried some Chinese medicine but it made no difference. In Hong Kong I brought some heavy duty intestinal worm medicine at around $10 US a pill, but they didn't stay in my guts long enough to do any good. When I got home I tried one heaped teaspoon of Diatomaceous Earth mixed with yogurt, and that slowed things down a lot. Then I tried mixing it with milk straight from the cow, and that put me back to square one. So I have to try something new, like go to the doctor. Anyway that is one of the joys of living in a developing country.

Epilogue

I never heard anything or whatever about what happened to Van. I couldn't get anyone on Facebook and I didn't know how to contact anyone in Hanoi. Anyway I made it back to Hanoi 6 months later and stayed in the same hostel. I got a different job at a different school and I kept going to the little garden in the mornings but I never saw Van again. A lot of the other street people who lived in the park or went to the park were there and most recognized me but since I couldn't speak the language I couldn't ask them what had happened to Van. The old woman was still there but I don't know if she recognized me as her mind was probably going but there was a vague something in her eyes when she saw me.

Anyway after six months I left again to head back to the West but I couldn't adapt back to civilization so I went back to Hanoi 6 months later and stayed there for another 6 months. I like the lifestyle and Hanoi, that's why I keep going back. This time I got another job at another school a bit further away from the hostel and the cathedral so I lived in a homestay in another part of Hanoi. One day as I was walking to work in the afternoon in about 30 something degree heat during the rainy season this guy on a bicycle in a raincoat with a hood on pulled up beside me and said "I don't know if you remember me" and it was Van. I couldn't believe it he lived around the corner from my school. He dragged me into his local coffee shop and we sat and had a chat. We used to meet there quite regularly as I went to that school nearly everyday. It was quite amazing really in a city of about 20 million people we bumped into each other on a small side road.

His story after I left. He lived in the garden and I don't know how he survived but someone took pity on him and got him a job as a security guard. So he was all set up, he had a job, a place to stay and money coming in so he was quite happy. I saw a lot of him this time until he moved away, his company sent him to another place and even then I used to go and visit him.

Because I had helped Van out when he was homeless he wouldn't let me buy anything, he would pay for the coffee and the cakes and whatever. Then he would get a motorcycle taxi and pay for it to take me home. Anyway my visa ran out so I had to leave and we missed each other on my last night in Hanoi. Six months later I went back to Hanoi but his phone had been disconnected so I couldn't contact him. Then the virus came along and I had to leave and so far I haven't been able to go back so I don't know what's happened to Van. As soon as flights resume and I can get out of here I'm heading back to Hanoi and I'll see if I can find him again.

Thank You For Your Time

Peter LeGrove

Make an Author Happy Today

If you found the material in this book helpful, I'd be eternally grateful if you took two minutes to write a review on Amazon. When you leave a review, it helps other readers find my books. Your review would make my day. Thank you!

- Go   to https://www.amazon.com/dp/B01L20URNG

- Scroll down to Customer Reviews

- Click on "Write a customer review" and do your thing. As long or as short as you like.

Thank you

Peter LeGrove

Other Books By Peter LeGrove

All my titles are available here
https://www.amazon.com/-/e/B00B8772MS

Teach and Travel in China

Live And Teach In Vietnam

Reading Student Struggling Student

Teach English as a Second Language to Children

How To Add Qualifications To Your CV Using FREE Courses

How To Make An Online CV Using Free Software

Survive and Thrive on the Road to your Future

Survive and Thrive on the Road to your Child's Future

Get Out Of Debt

Is Vegetable Gardening For You

Live Cheap in an UnCheap World

Is Civilization Collapse Happening Now

Are you Ready for Civilization Collapse

Teach A Man To Fish

How To Save Money

How To Lose Weight In An Over Weight World

How To NOT Live in the Toilet When You Have Stomach Parasites

Prepare Now To Survive Mother Nature's Wrath Or Mankind's Madness

Thank you and all the best on your Life Journey.
If you ever end up in a situation like I did I hope
this book will help you.

Peter Legrove

plegrove@gmail.com

www.animalsdinosaursandbugs.com

Live Cheap In An UnCheap World